Contents

Disclaimer

This book is intended for informational purposes only and is not a substitute for professional medical advice, diagnosis, or treatment. The contents of this book, including text, graphics, images, and other material ("Content"), are for informational purposes only. The Content is not intended to be a substitute for professional medical advice, diagnosis, or treatment. Always seek the advice of your physician or other qualified health provider with any questions you may have regarding a medical condition. Never disregard professional medical advice or delay in seeking it because of something you have read in this book.

The author of this book is not a medical professional, and the information provided in this book is based on the author's own research and personal understanding of Seasonal Affective Disorder (SAD). While efforts have been made to ensure the accuracy and completeness of the information presented, the author and publisher make no guarantees and disclaim any liability regarding the accuracy, completeness, or applicability of this information.

The author and publisher of this book shall not be liable for any direct, indirect, consequential, special, exemplary, or other damages arising therefrom. The information in this book is provided "as-is" and without warranties of any kind, either express or implied.

Readers are encouraged to confirm the information contained herein with other sources and to review the information carefully with their professional healthcare provider. The information is not intended to replace medical advice offered by physicians. The author and publisher of this book do not recommend or endorse any specific tests, physicians, products, procedures, opinions, or other information that may be mentioned in this book. Reliance on any information provided by this book is solely at your own risk.

Introduction

In the heart of winter, as the days shorten and the nights stretch long, a quiet change begins to take root in many of us. The vibrant energy of summer becomes a distant memory, and the world seems to slow down, wrapped in a cold, gray embrace. This change is not just in the world around us, but also within us, in the very ebb and flow of our emotions and energy levels. This is the world of seasonal depression, a subtle yet profound shift in our mental landscape guided by the rhythm of the seasons.

"Seasons of the Mind" is a journey into the heart of this phenomenon, known medically as Seasonal Affective Disorder (SAD). It's a tale not just of struggle and challenge, but also of understanding and hope. Through the pages of this book, we will explore how the changing seasons can dramatically alter our mood, behavior, and overall mental health. We will delve into personal stories, scientific research, and expert insights to uncover the hidden intricacies of this condition.

Seasonal depression is more than just "winter blues" or a fleeting sense of melancholy. For many, it is a recurring battle that arrives with the predictability of the changing leaves or the first snowfall. It can be debilitating, affecting work, relationships, and the simple act of getting through the day.

Yet, within this challenge lies the potential for profound growth and self-discovery. This book aims to illuminate the paths through the darker days, offering guidance and strategies to cope, and ultimately, to thrive. We will explore how light, both literal and metaphorical, can be a powerful ally against the shadow of seasonal depression. From light therapy to lifestyle changes, from cognitive-behavioral strategies to mindfulness and self-care, we will journey through a multitude of ways to bring balance back to our lives.

As you turn these pages, you may find echoes of your own experiences or those of someone close to you. "Seasons of the Mind" is not just a book; it's a companion for those cold, dark days and a guide towards a brighter, more balanced tomorrow. Welcome to a journey through the seasons of the mind, where every end is a new beginning, and the depths of winter can lead to the most profound springs.

Chapter 1 Understanding Seasonal Depression

Seasonal depression, clinically known as Seasonal Affective Disorder (SAD), is a type of depression that relates to changes in seasons. Unlike other forms of depression, SAD begins and ends at about the same times every year, with symptoms typically starting in the fall and continuing into the winter months, although a less common form can occur during the spring or early summer.

The Nature of Seasonal Depression

SAD is more than just the "winter blues" or a seasonal funk that someone can easily snap out of. It is a subtype of depression or bipolar disorder that occurs and ends at a specific time of year. The symptoms usually start mild and become more severe as the season progresses.

Symptoms of Seasonal Depression

Symptoms of the winter pattern of SAD might include:
-Feeling depressed most of the day, nearly every day
-Losing interest in activities you once enjoyed
-Low energy and increased sluggishness
-Difficulty sleeping or oversleeping
-Changes in appetite or weight (particularly a craving for foods high in carbohydrates)
-Feeling agitated or sluggish
-Difficulty concentrating
-Frequent thoughts of death or suicide

In contrast, the less common summer-onset SAD can involve symptoms such as insomnia, decreased appetite, weight loss, and agitation or anxiety.

Causes and Risk Factors

The specific cause of SAD remains unknown, though several factors might come into play:
-Reduced Sunlight: A decrease in sunlight can disrupt your body's internal clock and lead to feelings of depression.
-Serotonin Levels: Reduced sunlight can cause a drop in serotonin, a brain chemical (neurotransmitter) that affects mood.
-Melatonin Levels: The change in season can disrupt the balance of the body's melatonin levels, which play a role in sleep patterns and mood.

Risk factors for SAD include:
-Being female: SAD is diagnosed more often in women than in men, but men may have more severe symptoms.

-Living far from the equator: SAD is more common among people who live far north or south of the equator.

-Family history: Having relatives with other types of depression increases the risk of SAD.

-Having depression or bipolar disorder: Symptoms of depression may worsen seasonally if you have one of these conditions.

How SAD Differs from Other Forms of Depression

While SAD is a type of depression, there are key differences:

-Seasonality: The most distinguishing feature of SAD is the clear onset and end of episodes in alignment with specific seasons.

-Symptom Patterns: The symptoms specific to winter SAD, such as increased sleep, appetite, and weight, are in contrast to typical depression symptoms, which often involve insomnia and loss of appetite.

-Light Sensitivity: People with SAD are often particularly sensitive to light, or lack thereof, which is not a common feature in other types of depression.

Chapter 2 The Science Behind the Seasons

In this chapter, we delve into the science underlying Seasonal Affective Disorder (SAD), understanding how and why the changing seasons can so profoundly affect our mood and mental health.

The Role of Light in Our Lives

The amount of daylight we receive has a significant impact on our internal biological clocks, or circadian rhythms. These rhythms are critical in determining our sleep patterns, and they influence various other physiological processes, including hormone release, body temperature, and metabolism. When there's less daylight, our circadian rhythms can get out of sync, affecting our overall mood and well-being.

Sunlight and Serotonin

Sunlight directly influences the production of serotonin, a neurotransmitter that contributes to feelings of well-being and happiness. Reduced sunlight in fall and winter can lead to a drop in serotonin, potentially triggering depression. The change in season can affect serotonin levels by altering the serotonin transporter, leading to lower neurotransmitter levels in the brain.

Melatonin and Its Effects

Melatonin is a hormone produced in the pineal gland that responds to darkness, helping regulate sleep and mood. When the days are shorter and darker, the production of melatonin increases, potentially causing lethargy and symptoms of depression.

Vitamin D and Its Role in Mental Health

Vitamin D, widely known as the "sunshine vitamin," holds a crucial place in the discussion about mental health, particularly in relation to Seasonal Affective Disorder (SAD). Our skin synthesizes this essential vitamin upon exposure to sunlight, specifically UVB rays. This process highlights the direct connection between sunlight exposure and our physiological well-being.

The role of Vitamin D in regulating mood, especially its involvement in serotonin activity, is a key area of interest. Serotonin, a neurotransmitter often dubbed the 'feel-good chemical,' plays a significant role in stabilizing mood, feelings of well-being, and happiness. Research indicates that Vitamin D helps in the conversion of tryptophan into serotonin. This means that lower levels of Vitamin D, particularly common in the darker winter months, could lead to decreased serotonin production, potentially contributing to the depressive symptoms often seen in SAD.

The link between Vitamin D deficiency and depression has been a subject of various studies. Individuals with lower levels of Vitamin D have been found to be at a higher risk of developing depressive symptoms. These symptoms can be particularly pronounced in individuals suffering from SAD,

given the reduced sunlight exposure during winter. In regions far from the equator where sunlight is scarce during certain times of the year, the prevalence of SAD and Vitamin D deficiency-related depressive symptoms is notably higher.

It's not just the lack of sunlight that contributes to Vitamin D deficiency; lifestyle factors like spending more time indoors, using sunscreen excessively, or wearing clothing that covers most of the skin can also limit Vitamin D synthesis. In such cases, dietary sources of Vitamin D – such as fatty fish, egg yolks, and fortified foods – become particularly important. For some, especially those living in areas with limited winter sunlight, Vitamin D supplementation might be necessary. However, it is important to consult with a healthcare professional before starting any supplement, as Vitamin D levels can be accurately assessed through a blood test and supplementation needs can vary greatly among individuals.

In conclusion, Vitamin D's relationship with serotonin and its subsequent impact on mood underscores its importance in the context of SAD. Ensuring adequate Vitamin D levels, whether through sunlight exposure, diet, or supplements, can be a key component in managing and potentially alleviating the depressive symptoms associated with this condition.

Genetic Factors

Recent advancements in the study of Seasonal Affective Disorder (SAD) have shed light on the potential genetic underpinnings of this condition, suggesting that genetics may play a more significant role than previously understood. These studies propose that certain individuals may have a genetic predisposition to SAD, making them more susceptible to its symptoms than others. This genetic link can be a critical factor in understanding why SAD appears to be more prevalent in some families, indicating a hereditary pattern in the susceptibility to this disorder.

The hypothesis of a genetic component in SAD aligns with broader research in the field of mood disorders, where genetic factors are often found to contribute to the likelihood of developing conditions like depression and bipolar disorder. In the case of SAD, researchers are exploring specific genetic markers that could influence the body's regulation of circadian rhythms, serotonin pathways, and the processing of Vitamin D – all of which are crucial elements in the onset and progression of SAD. Circadian rhythms, which are often disrupted in SAD patients, are partially regulated by genetic factors. Hence, variations in these genes might lead to a higher vulnerability to the seasonal changes that trigger SAD symptoms.

Furthermore, familial studies and twin studies have provided more evidence supporting the genetic basis of SAD. These studies have shown a higher concordance rate for SAD among monozygotic (identical) twins compared to dizygotic (fraternal) twins, further suggesting a genetic influence.

However, it's important to note that genetics are just one piece of the puzzle. Environmental factors, such as latitude, climate, and individual lifestyle choices, also play a significant role in the development of SAD. For instance, individuals living in higher latitudes with less winter sunlight have higher rates of SAD, regardless of genetic predisposition.

The understanding that a genetic component may contribute to SAD is a significant step forward in unraveling the complexities of this disorder. It not only helps in identifying those at higher risk but also paves the way for more personalized treatment approaches. As research continues to evolve, it may lead to more targeted therapies that take into account both the genetic and environmental factors contributing to SAD, offering more effective management and treatment strategies for those affected.

The Impact of Climate and Geography

The prevalence of SAD varies significantly with latitude, altitude, and climate, suggesting a strong environmental component. For example, it is more common in the northern regions of the United States and in countries far from the equator where daylight hours in winter are very short.

Differentiating SAD from Other Mental Health Disorders

While SAD shares many symptoms with other forms of depression, its seasonal pattern is unique. It's also distinct from conditions like bipolar disorder, though it can exacerbate these conditions.

The science behind SAD is complex and involves an interplay of biological and environmental factors. This chapter underscores the importance of light, both natural and artificial, in regulating our mood and physiological processes. As we progress, the subsequent chapters will explore how we can harness this understanding to mitigate the symptoms of SAD and improve our mental health during the challenging seasons.

Chapter 3 Personal Stories

In this chapter, we turn our attention to the personal experiences of those who have been touched by Seasonal Affective Disorder (SAD). By sharing these stories, we gain a deeper, more human understanding of how SAD affects individuals in their daily lives. These narratives provide insight into the struggle, resilience, and hope that characterize living with this condition.

Story 1: Emma's Winter Silence

Emma, a 32-year-old graphic designer, had always relished the change of seasons. The vibrant fall colors, the first snowfall, and the cozy winter nights were things she looked forward to every year. But a few years ago, she noticed a change in herself as the days grew shorter and the nights longer.

It started subtly. Emma found herself feeling less enthusiastic about her weekend hiking trips. The hobbies that once filled her with joy, like painting and photography, no longer seemed appealing. At first, she attributed this decline in interest to the natural ebb and flow of life's passions. However, as winter approached, her energy levels plummeted. The zest for life she once felt was replaced by an overwhelming sense of fatigue and lethargy.

Each morning, waking up felt like a herculean task. Emma, once a morning person, now struggled to leave the warmth of her bed. The world outside her window, blanketed in snow, seemed detached and colorless. Her work, which had always been a source of pride and fulfillment, became a source of anxiety. Deadlines that were once easily met now loomed over her like insurmountable mountains.

At first, Emma kept her struggles to herself. She felt ashamed, unable to understand why she, who had everything seemingly going right, should feel so down. Social gatherings became a chore. She started avoiding friends, giving excuses to skip outings, and spending weekends curled up in bed.

It was during a video call with her sister, who lived in sunny California, that Emma first heard the term "Seasonal Affective Disorder." Her sister noticed Emma's lackluster appearance and muted energy and suggested she read about it. Reluctantly, Emma did, and with each symptom she read, a lightbulb went off in her head. The fatigue, the depression during winter months, the loss of interest in activities she loved – it all resonated with her.

Accepting that she might be facing SAD was both a relief and a challenge for Emma. She reached out for professional help, starting therapy with a counselor who specialized in mood disorders. Together, they worked on a treatment plan that included light therapy, a structured daily routine, and cognitive-behavioral strategies to manage negative thoughts.

Emma also made lifestyle changes. She started a regular indoor exercise routine and made a conscious effort to socialize, even when her mind urged her to withdraw. She learned to be open about her struggles with friends and family, finding comfort in their support and understanding.

Winter still poses a challenge for Emma, but she now approaches it with awareness and tools to help manage her symptoms. She has rekindled her love for painting, often using it as a therapeutic tool to express her emotions. Her journey hasn't been easy, but it has been transformative. Emma's story is a testament to the power of understanding, the importance of seeking help, and the strength of the human spirit in the face of seasonal darkness.

Story 2: David's Summers of Discontent

David, a 40-year-old high school teacher, always dreaded the onset of summer. Unlike most of his colleagues and students who eagerly anticipated the warm, sunny months, David experienced a profound sense of unease as the days lengthened. His story is an exploration of summer-onset Seasonal Affective Disorder (SAD), a lesser-known but equally impactful variant of the condition.

For David, the arrival of summer brought sleepless nights and a restless mind. The extended daylight hours, which energized others, seemed to drain him. He felt a constant state of agitation, his thoughts racing faster than he could process them. His appetite diminished, and with it, his energy levels plummeted.

Initially, David struggled to understand what was happening to him. Summer is traditionally associated with happiness and relaxation, but for him, it was a period of anxiety and turmoil. He found himself becoming irritable, snapping at minor inconveniences, a stark contrast to his usual calm and patient demeanor.

His troubles began to spill over into his professional life. Grading papers became a daunting task, and his usual passion for teaching and engaging with students waned. The isolation he felt was profound; after all, who struggles with depression during summer?

It was during a routine medical check-up that David first broached the subject of his summer struggles with his doctor. The doctor suggested that David might be experiencing summer-onset SAD, a suggestion that initially left him incredulous. However, as they discussed the symptoms, David recognized the patterns in his own life.

Acknowledging the problem was David's first step towards managing it. He sought the help of a therapist who specialized in mood disorders and began a treatment plan tailored to his needs. Cognitive-behavioral therapy (CBT) helped him manage his anxiety and negative thought patterns. His therapist also recommended spending some time in darker, cooler environments to help mitigate the overstimulation caused by the extended daylight.

David made lifestyle adjustments as well. He began practicing mindfulness and meditation to calm his restless mind. To combat his insomnia, he established a strict bedtime routine and made his bedroom a cool, dark sanctuary for sleep. Engaging in regular, moderate exercise, especially in the early mornings or evenings when the sun was less intense, also became an integral part of his routine.

One of the most significant changes for David was learning to be open about his condition. He found support in online communities where others shared his experiences with summer SAD. This connection was vital in normalizing his experience and reducing the isolation he felt.

David's journey with summer-onset SAD is a reminder that mental health disorders can take many forms and don't always fit into conventional expectations. By sharing his story, David hopes to raise awareness about this lesser-known form of SAD and to offer hope to others who might be silently struggling during the summer months.

Story 3: The Johnson Family's Collective Struggle

The Johnson family's story is a poignant illustration of how Seasonal Affective Disorder (SAD) can impact not just the individual suffering from it but the entire family dynamic. This narrative centers around Susan, a devoted mother and wife, whose battle with SAD brought unexpected challenges and lessons to her family.

Susan, known for her vibrant personality and active lifestyle, began to experience significant mood changes as the days shortened. Her husband, Mark, and their two teenage children, Lily and Ethan, were initially puzzled by the shift in her behavior. The energetic and attentive mother and wife they knew seemed to retreat into a shell as winter approached. She lost interest in family activities, struggled with fatigue, and became increasingly irritable and withdrawn.

The change was gradual but undeniable. Household responsibilities started to slip, and Susan's absence was felt in every corner of their home life. Mark found himself juggling his job and additional household duties, while Lily and Ethan grappled with the confusion and worry about their mother's well-being.

It was during a parent-teacher meeting that a teacher, who had known the family for years, expressed concern about Susan's drastic change in demeanor. She suggested that Susan might be experiencing more than just stress or the typical winter blues. This conversation was a turning point, prompting the family to seek medical advice.

After a thorough evaluation, Susan was diagnosed with Seasonal Affective Disorder. The diagnosis brought a mix of emotions to the family: relief in having an explanation, concern about the condition, and uncertainty about what it meant for their future.

The family embarked on a journey of learning and adaptation. They attended therapy sessions together, where they learned about SAD and how to support Susan. Mark and the children became more involved in household management, easing Susan's burden. They also learned to recognize and anticipate the signs of her mood shifts, adapting their family routines accordingly.

One of the most significant changes was in their home environment. They introduced light therapy in their daily routine, placed more emphasis on outdoor activities during daylight hours, and restructured their living space to maximize natural light. These changes, seemingly small, had a profound impact on Susan's mood and, by extension, on the family's overall well-being.

Through this experience, Lily and Ethan learned valuable lessons in empathy and resilience. They became more independent and understanding, qualities that extended beyond their home life. Mark, who had initially felt helpless, found strength in being a pillar of support for his wife and children.

The Johnson family's story is a testament to the power of understanding, adaptability, and collective support in facing the challenges posed by SAD. Their journey highlights the importance of family in mental health and the strength that can be found in facing challenges together.

Chapter 4: Diagnosis and Recognition

In this chapter, we explore the critical steps of diagnosing Seasonal Affective Disorder (SAD) and the importance of recognizing its symptoms. Proper diagnosis and awareness are key to managing this condition effectively.

Understanding the Symptoms

The first step in diagnosing SAD is recognizing its symptoms. Unlike other forms of depression, the symptoms of SAD are closely tied to seasonal changes. Common symptoms include:

-Depressive mood

-Loss of interest in previously enjoyable activities

-Changes in appetite or weight

-Sleep disturbances (oversleeping in winter SAD, insomnia in summer SAD)

-Fatigue or low energy

-Feelings of hopelessness or worthlessness

-Difficulty concentrating

-Thoughts of death or suicide

-The Seasonal Pattern

A distinctive feature of SAD is its seasonal pattern. Symptoms typically begin in the fall and continue into the winter months, subsiding during the spring and summer. In less common cases, individuals may experience symptoms during the late spring or early summer that resolve during the fall and winter.

Differential Diagnosis

Diagnosing SAD involves differentiating it from other types of depression or mental health conditions. Healthcare providers consider various factors, including the timing and duration of symptoms, family and personal mental health history, and the impact of symptoms on daily functioning.

Diagnostic Criteria

The American Psychiatric Association's Diagnostic and Statistical Manual of Mental Disorders (DSM-5) provides criteria for diagnosing SAD as a type of depression with a seasonal pattern. Key criteria include:

Presence of major depression coinciding with specific seasons for at least two consecutive years.

Seasonal depressions substantially outnumber non-seasonal depressive episodes throughout the individual's lifetime.

The Role of Medical Professionals

Diagnosis is typically made by a mental health professional or a primary care provider. A thorough evaluation may include a physical examination, laboratory tests (to rule out other medical conditions that can mimic depression), and detailed discussions about mental health and lifestyle.

Self-Assessment and Awareness

The role of self-assessment tools and heightened awareness in the context of Seasonal Affective Disorder (SAD) is pivotal in facilitating early detection and intervention, which are key elements for effective management of the disorder. Recognizing the onset of SAD can be challenging, as its symptoms often mimic those of other types of depression or may be mistaken for the common 'winter blues.' However, unlike typical mood fluctuations, SAD is characterized by recurrent patterns of depression corresponding with specific seasons, primarily the winter months. Self-assessment tools, which often include questionnaires and checklists focused on the frequency, severity, and duration of specific symptoms, can be instrumental in helping individuals discern whether their experiences align with SAD.

Awareness about the nature and symptoms of SAD is equally crucial. This includes understanding that SAD is not just about feeling down during winter but is a recognized form of depression with a seasonal pattern. Symptoms such as persistent low mood, loss of interest in usually pleasurable activities, changes in appetite or sleep patterns, lethargy, and feelings of despair are all red flags. By increasing awareness, individuals are more likely to notice these patterns in themselves or others and understand the importance of seeking professional help.

Early intervention is a critical aspect of managing SAD effectively. The sooner the symptoms are recognized and addressed, the better the chances are for a positive treatment outcome. Timely intervention can prevent symptoms from escalating to a more severe state and can help in maintaining normal functioning in personal and professional life. Treatment options such as light therapy, cognitive behavioral therapy, and lifestyle modifications are more effective when initiated early in the course of the disorder.

Additionally, awareness and self-assessment can help in breaking down the stigma associated with SAD and mental health disorders in general. By understanding that SAD is a medical condition that can be effectively managed with appropriate treatment, individuals are more likely to seek and adhere to treatment without the burden of social stigma.

Finally, self-assessment tools and increased awareness play a critical role in the early detection and management of SAD. They empower individuals to take an active role in recognizing the symptoms and seeking professional help, thereby enabling earlier and more effective intervention. These tools not only aid in individual health but also contribute to broader public awareness, fostering a more informed and supportive approach to dealing with Seasonal Affective Disorder.

Importance of Early Recognition

Early recognition and diagnosis are vital. SAD can impact quality of life, personal relationships, and job performance. Timely intervention can prevent symptoms from worsening and reduce the overall impact of the disorder.

Recognizing and accurately diagnosing Seasonal Affective Disorder is essential for effective treatment and management. This chapter underscores the importance of being aware of the symptoms of SAD, understanding its unique seasonal patterns, and seeking professional help for diagnosis and treatment. As we move forward, we will delve into various treatment strategies and lifestyle adjustments that can help manage SAD effectively.

Chapter 5: Light Therapy

In Chapter 5, we delve into one of the most effective and widely used treatments for Seasonal Affective Disorder (SAD) - Light Therapy. This chapter explains what light therapy is, how it works, and how to integrate it effectively into a treatment plan for SAD.

Understanding Light Therapy

Light therapy, or phototherapy, stands as a cornerstone in the treatment of Seasonal Affective Disorder (SAD), a condition where diminished sunlight in the winter months can lead to significant mood alterations and depressive symptoms. This therapy harnesses the power of a specially designed artificial light to mimic the natural outdoor light that's often lacking during the shorter days of the year. When undergoing light therapy, individuals are exposed to a light box emitting bright light, much brighter than typical indoor lighting, but filtered to remove UV rays, making it safe for regular use.

The underlying mechanism of how light therapy exerts its beneficial effects in SAD is rooted in the intricate relationship between light exposure and our brain's chemistry. Sunlight plays a pivotal role in regulating various biological processes, including the circadian rhythms — our internal biological clock — that govern sleep-wake cycles and hormonal release. During the darker months, these rhythms can become disrupted, leading to changes in mood and energy levels. Light therapy works by effectively resetting these circadian rhythms, thereby improving sleep patterns, energy levels, and overall mood.

Moreover, exposure to bright light has been shown to trigger a chemical change in the brain. It stimulates the production of serotonin, a neurotransmitter often referred to as the 'feel-good' hormone due to its mood-boosting effects. This is particularly relevant in the context of SAD, where reduced sunlight can lead to a decrease in serotonin levels, contributing to feelings of depression. The light from the therapy boxes is believed to increase serotonin production, helping to alleviate depressive symptoms associated with SAD.

The effectiveness of light therapy is most pronounced when it is used consistently, typically as part of a daily routine. Most users sit in front of the light box for about 20 to 30 minutes each day, preferably in the morning, to mimic the sunrise and kickstart the circadian rhythm cycle. This routine can lead to significant improvements in mood, concentration, and energy levels, often within a few days to a few weeks of starting the therapy.

In conclusion, light therapy represents a significant advancement in the treatment of Seasonal Affective Disorder, offering a non-invasive, medication-free method to alleviate its symptoms. By simulating the effects of natural sunlight, light therapy addresses the root of the problem in SAD, realigning the body's internal clock and improving brain chemistry, which can lead to substantial improvements in the mental well-being of individuals affected by this seasonal condition.

The Science Behind Light Therapy

The exact mechanism of how light therapy works in treating SAD is not fully understood, but it is believed to affect brain chemicals linked to mood, possibly easing SAD symptoms. It's thought to stimulate serotonin production while regulating melatonin, which helps reset the body's internal clock or circadian rhythm.

Types of Light Therapy Devices

Light Boxes: These are flat screens that produce full-spectrum fluorescent light, usually at an intensity of 10,000 lux.

Dawn Simulators: These devices mimic a natural sunrise by gradually increasing the amount of light in a room over a set period.

Light Visors: These portable devices are worn on the head and offer more mobility.

Effective Use of Light Therapy

Timing: The most effective time to use a light box is in the morning, shortly after waking up.

Duration: Treatment typically involves daily sessions ranging from 20 to 60 minutes.

Consistency: Regular use of light therapy is crucial, as symptoms can return if it's discontinued or used inconsistently.

Choosing the Right Device

When choosing a light therapy device, it's important to ensure it filters out UV rays and provides the desired intensity of light. Consulting with a healthcare provider can help determine the best option.

Potential Side Effects

While light therapy is generally safe, it can have side effects, including eyestrain, headache, nausea, irritability, or agitation. People with certain medical conditions or taking specific medications should discuss potential risks with their doctor.

Combining Light Therapy with Other Treatments

Light therapy is often used in conjunction with other treatments, such as psychotherapy or medication. The combination of treatments can often provide the most effective relief from SAD symptoms.

Light therapy is a cornerstone in the treatment of Seasonal Affective Disorder. Its ease of use, coupled with its effectiveness, makes it an invaluable tool in managing SAD symptoms. However, it is not a one-size-fits-all solution, and working with healthcare professionals to tailor a treatment plan is crucial. The next chapters will explore additional treatments and lifestyle changes that can complement light therapy and further aid in managing SAD.

Chapter 6: Nutrition and Exercise

In Chapter 6, we explore the vital roles of nutrition and exercise in managing Seasonal Affective Disorder (SAD). A balanced diet and regular physical activity can significantly impact overall mood and energy levels, proving to be powerful tools in combating the symptoms of SAD.

Nutritional Considerations for SAD

Diet plays a crucial role in mental health. Certain nutrients are particularly important for those suffering from SAD:

-Omega-3 Fatty Acids: Found in fish, flaxseeds, and walnuts, omega-3s are linked to improved brain health and mood regulation.

-Vitamin D: Low levels of vitamin D are associated with depressive symptoms. With limited sunlight in winter, supplementing vitamin D or consuming vitamin D-rich foods like fatty fish, egg yolks, and fortified products can be beneficial.

-Complex Carbohydrates: Whole grains, fruits, and vegetables can boost serotonin levels and stabilize blood sugar, impacting mood and energy.

-Lean Proteins: Sources like chicken, turkey, and legumes provide amino acids essential for neurotransmitter function, which can influence mood.

-B Vitamins: Particularly B12 and folate, found in leafy greens, legumes, and fortified cereals, are important for brain health and mood regulation.

The Impact of Diet on Mood

What we eat can have a significant impact on our mood. A diet high in processed foods, sugar, and caffeine can exacerbate symptoms of SAD by causing fluctuations in blood sugar levels and affecting brain function.

Understanding the Brain-Gut Connection

Recent research has highlighted the importance of the gut-brain axis – the bidirectional communication pathway between the gastrointestinal tract and the brain. This connection means that the state of our gut health can directly impact our mental health. A diet that promotes a healthy gut microbiome, therefore, can positively influence brain function and mood.

The Effects of Processed Foods, Sugar, and Caffeine

-Processed Foods: These foods often contain additives, preservatives, and artificial ingredients that can disrupt the balance of gut bacteria. They are also typically high in refined carbohydrates and trans fats, which can lead to inflammation – a condition increasingly linked to mood disorders.

-Sugar: High sugar consumption can lead to fluctuations in blood sugar levels. These fluctuations can trigger mood swings and irritability. Over time, excessive sugar intake can also lead to inflammation and increase the risk of developing depression.

-Caffeine: While caffeine can temporarily boost alertness and mood, overconsumption can lead to increased anxiety, sleep disturbances, and mood swings, especially in individuals sensitive to caffeine or those with existing mood disorders.

Nutritional Strategies for Managing Mood

-Balanced Diet: Eating a diet rich in whole foods such as fruits, vegetables, whole grains, lean proteins, and healthy fats can provide essential nutrients that support brain health and stabilize mood. These foods are rich in antioxidants, vitamins, and minerals that combat inflammation and support neurotransmitter function.

-Complex Carbohydrates: Foods like whole grains, legumes, and vegetables provide a steady source of energy, helping to maintain stable blood sugar levels and mood.

-Omega-3 Fatty Acids: Found in fatty fish, flaxseeds, and walnuts, omega-3s are crucial for brain health and have been shown to improve symptoms of depression.

-Probiotics and Prebiotics: These support a healthy gut microbiome, which is essential for brain health. Fermented foods like yogurt, kefir, kombucha, and sauerkraut are rich in probiotics, while prebiotics are found in foods like garlic, onions, and asparagus.

-Adequate Hydration: As mentioned previously, staying hydrated is essential for maintaining optimal brain function and mood.

-Limiting Alcohol: Alcohol can affect neurotransmitter balance and mood. It can also disrupt sleep, which is crucial for mental health.

The Role of Individual Nutrients in Mood Regulation

-Vitamin D: Often referred to as the 'sunshine vitamin,' Vitamin D deficiency has been linked to increased risk of depression. Considering that SAD is partly triggered by reduced sunlight exposure, ensuring adequate Vitamin D levels is crucial.

-B Vitamins: Particularly B12 and folate, play a vital role in brain health and are linked to reduced depression and anxiety.

-Magnesium: This mineral is vital for brain function and is known for its calming effects on the nervous system.

Exercise and SAD

Regular physical activity is a powerful antidote to depression, including SAD. Exercise not only promotes overall health but also releases endorphins and serotonin, which can improve mood and energy levels.

Outdoor Exercise: Whenever possible, exercising outdoors during daylight hours maximizes light exposure, enhancing the mood-boosting benefits.

Types of Exercise: Aerobic exercises like walking, running, swimming, or cycling are particularly effective. However, any form of exercise, from yoga to weight training, can be beneficial.

Frequency and Duration: Consistency is key. Most benefits are observed with regular exercise, ideally most days of the week for at least 30 minutes.

The Role of Hydration

Water is essential for every cell in the body, including brain cells. Proper hydration is crucial for maintaining optimal brain function and chemical balance. When the body is dehydrated, it can lead to reduced blood flow to the brain, which in turn can cause cognitive difficulties such as problems with focus, memory, and decision-making. These cognitive impairments can exacerbate the symptoms of depression and anxiety often associated with SAD.

Dehydration can have a direct impact on mood. Studies have shown that even mild dehydration can lead to irritability, lack of concentration, and a decrease in mental alertness, which can worsen the symptoms of SAD. Moreover, dehydration can stress the body, and when the body is stressed, mental health symptoms can become more pronounced.

Staying Hydrated: Tips and Strategies

Consistent Fluid Intake: It's important to drink water consistently throughout the day, not just when you feel thirsty. Thirst is often a late sign of dehydration.

Monitor Hydration Levels: Pay attention to the color of your urine. Pale and clear urine is a good sign of hydration, while dark-colored urine can indicate dehydration.

Incorporate Foods with High Water Content: Fruits and vegetables like cucumbers, lettuce, melons, and berries can help maintain hydration levels.

Limit Diuretics: Beverages like coffee, tea, and alcohol can have diuretic effects, leading to increased fluid loss. Moderation is key, and it's important to balance these beverages with water intake.

Setting Hydration Goals: Having a daily water intake goal can be helpful. Tools like hydration tracking apps or marked water bottles can help in reaching these goals.

Hydration and Exercise: When exercising, especially during physical activities that can cause heavy sweating, it's crucial to drink enough water to compensate for the fluid loss.

Creating a Balanced Lifestyle

Integrating a healthy diet and regular exercise into one's lifestyle is about more than managing symptoms of SAD; it's about creating a foundation for overall mental and physical well-being.

Nutrition and exercise play pivotal roles in the management of SAD. By making conscious choices about diet and maintaining an active lifestyle, individuals with SAD can significantly improve their symptoms and overall quality of life. In the next chapters, we will look at other lifestyle adjustments and therapeutic approaches that complement these fundamental strategies.

Chapter 7: Cognitive-Behavioral Strategies

In Chapter 7, we focus on Cognitive-Behavioral Therapy (CBT) and its application in managing Seasonal Affective Disorder (SAD). CBT is a widely used therapeutic approach that helps individuals change negative thought patterns and behaviors, which can be particularly beneficial for those with SAD.

Understanding Cognitive-Behavioral Therapy

CBT is based on the concept that our thoughts, feelings, and behaviors are interconnected, and that changing negative thought patterns can lead to changes in feelings and behaviors. This approach is particularly effective in treating depression, including SAD.

CBT Techniques for SAD

Identifying Negative Thoughts: Individuals learn to recognize and challenge the automatic negative thoughts that contribute to depressive feelings.

Behavioral Activation: This involves identifying activities that are enjoyable or fulfilling and incorporating them into daily routines, countering the tendency to withdraw and become inactive during depressive episodes.

Cognitive Restructuring: This technique helps to challenge and change irrational beliefs and negative thinking patterns into more positive, realistic thoughts.

Mindfulness and Acceptance: Mindfulness-based cognitive therapy combines mindfulness techniques like meditation with CBT to increase awareness and acceptance of thoughts and feelings without judgment.

Using CBT to Combat SAD

Light Exposure: Integrating light therapy with CBT, individuals can learn to associate light exposure with positive cognitive and behavioral changes.

Scheduling Activities: Planning and engaging in activities, especially during the most challenging times of the year, can help maintain a positive mood and energy levels.

Journaling: Keeping a journal can be a powerful tool for self-reflection and for tracking thoughts, moods, and progress.

CBT and Lifestyle Adjustments

CBT often works best in conjunction with lifestyle changes, such as improved diet, regular exercise, and adequate sleep. These changes can reinforce the cognitive and behavioral shifts achieved through therapy.

Professional Guidance

While there are self-help resources available for CBT, working with a trained therapist can provide tailored guidance and support, which is often more effective, especially for those new to CBT.

Cognitive-Behavioral Therapy is a powerful tool in the management of SAD. By addressing the cognitive aspects of the disorder, CBT provides strategies to cope with and alleviate symptoms. Alongside other treatments like light therapy and medication, CBT can significantly improve quality of life for individuals with SAD. Upcoming chapters will explore additional therapeutic modalities and how they can be integrated into a comprehensive treatment plan.

Chapter 8: The Role of Medication

In Chapter 8, we delve into the role of medication in the treatment of Seasonal Affective Disorder (SAD). While lifestyle changes and therapies like light therapy and Cognitive-Behavioral Therapy (CBT) are effective, some cases of SAD may require pharmacological intervention for optimal management.

Understanding When Medication is Needed

Medication for SAD is typically considered when symptoms are severe, have a significant impact on daily functioning, or when other treatment methods have not provided sufficient relief. The decision to use medication should be made in consultation with a healthcare professional, taking into account the individual's medical history, symptom severity, and personal preferences.

Common Medications for SAD

Selective Serotonin Reuptake Inhibitors (SSRIs): These are the most commonly prescribed type of antidepressants for SAD. They work by increasing levels of serotonin in the brain. Examples include fluoxetine (Prozac), sertraline (Zoloft), and citalopram (Celexa).

Bupropion XL: This is an antidepressant that's specifically approved for the prevention of major depressive episodes in patients with SAD. It's unique in that it affects both norepinephrine and dopamine neurotransmitters.

Timing and Duration of Medication

Preventive Use: For some individuals, starting medication before the onset of the SAD season (usually in early fall) and continuing through the winter months can prevent the development of symptoms.

Duration of Use: The duration of medication use can vary from person to person. Some may need it only during the SAD season, while others might continue it year-round to prevent recurrence.

Monitoring and Side Effects

It's important to be monitored regularly by a healthcare provider while taking medication for SAD to assess the effectiveness and manage any side effects.

Common side effects of SSRIs include nausea, insomnia, anxiety, restlessness, and decreased libido. Bupropion may cause dry mouth, headache, constipation, and increased heart rate.

Medication in Combination with Other Treatments

Medication is often most effective when combined with other treatments like light therapy, CBT, and lifestyle changes. This multifaceted approach can address various aspects of SAD, leading to better outcomes.

Alternative Medications

In some cases, other types of antidepressants or mood stabilizers may be prescribed, depending on the individual's specific symptoms and medical history.

Medication can play a crucial role in the treatment of SAD for some individuals. It's important to approach medication as part of a comprehensive treatment plan, tailored to the individual's needs and monitored by healthcare professionals. The subsequent chapters will explore additional complementary therapies and the importance of a holistic approach to managing SAD.

Chapter 9: Alternative Therapies

In Chapter 9, we explore various alternative therapies that can be used alongside more traditional treatments for Seasonal Affective Disorder (SAD). These therapies can offer additional relief and can be particularly appealing for those seeking holistic or complementary approaches.

Aromatherapy

Essential oils like lavender, bergamot, and ylang-ylang can have mood-boosting effects.

Aromatherapy can be used through diffusers, personal inhalers, or topical application.

Herbal Remedies

Certain herbs like St. John's Wort and SAM-e are known for their mood-enhancing properties.

It's crucial to discuss with a healthcare provider before using herbal supplements, especially if you're taking other medications.

Acupuncture

This traditional Chinese medicine technique involves inserting thin needles into specific body points. It is believed to correct imbalances in the body's energy flow (Qi), potentially helping with depressive symptoms.

Light and Color Therapy

Beyond standard light therapy, color therapy (or chromotherapy) uses various colors to alter mood and emotional health. Each color is thought to have different healing properties.

Mindfulness and Meditation

Practices such as meditation, yoga, and tai chi can improve mental well-being, reduce stress, and help manage symptoms of depression.

Naturopathy

Naturopathic doctors can provide personalized advice on diet, exercise, and natural supplements to manage SAD symptoms.

Music and Art Therapy

Engaging in creative activities like music and art can be therapeutic and offer an emotional outlet for those suffering from SAD.

Alternative therapies can be valuable additions to a treatment plan for SAD. They often work best when used in conjunction with traditional treatments like light therapy and medication. The effectiveness of these therapies can vary from person to person, and it's important to consult with healthcare professionals when integrating new treatments.

Chapter 10: Maintaining Social Connections

In Chapter 10, we focus on the importance of maintaining social connections and support systems in managing Seasonal Affective Disorder (SAD). Isolation can exacerbate symptoms of SAD, making social interaction a key component in its management.

Understanding the Impact of Socialization

The role of social interactions in managing Seasonal Affective Disorder (SAD) is both significant and multifaceted. For individuals grappling with SAD, the tendency to withdraw and isolate can be strong, particularly during the peak of the disorder in the colder, darker months. However, engaging in social activities can be a powerful antidote to the feelings of loneliness and seclusion that often accompany this condition. Interacting with others can serve as a mood booster, lifting spirits and providing a sense of connectedness that is essential for emotional well-being.

Social connections provide a platform for emotional support, allowing individuals to share their experiences, express their feelings, and gain perspective from others. This exchange can be incredibly validating and reassuring, particularly for those who might otherwise feel misunderstood or alone in their struggle with SAD. The simple act of conversing with friends, participating in group activities, or even engaging in brief social interactions in day-to-day life can trigger the release of neurotransmitters like endorphins and oxytocin, which are known to enhance mood and promote feelings of happiness and well-being.

Moreover, maintaining social connections can also serve as a buffer against the stress and anxiety that often accompany SAD. Social support has been shown to play a role in resilience to stress, helping individuals to better manage and cope with the challenges they face. Engaging in social activities can also provide a distraction from the symptoms of SAD, offering a change of pace and environment that can break the cycle of negative thoughts and feelings.

Importantly, social interactions can also play a role in encouraging healthy behaviors and routines, which are crucial in managing SAD. Friends and family can motivate one another to stay active, get outside, and engage in activities that might otherwise be neglected during periods of low mood. They can also serve as a source of accountability, helping to ensure that individuals stick to treatment plans and self-care routines.

Lastly, social interactions are a key component in managing Seasonal Affective Disorder. They provide emotional support, enhance mood, and encourage behaviors that contribute to overall well-being. While it can be challenging for those with SAD to seek out and engage in social activities, doing so can have a profound and positive impact on their ability to manage the condition effectively.

Strategies for Social Engagement

Scheduled Socializing: Plan regular activities with friends or family, even if it's a simple weekly phone call or coffee meet-up.

Support Groups: Joining a SAD support group can provide a sense of community and understanding.

Volunteering: Engaging in volunteer work can offer a sense of purpose and connection.

Communicating with Loved Ones

Open communication with friends and family about your experience with SAD can help them understand how to offer support.

Using Technology to Stay Connected

In the contemporary landscape where technology permeates nearly every aspect of life, digital platforms have become increasingly vital in maintaining social connections, especially for those managing Seasonal Affective Disorder (SAD). Video calls, social media, and various other online platforms have emerged as crucial tools in bridging the gap created by physical distance or the challenges posed by the symptoms of SAD, which often make in-person interactions difficult.

Video calls, through platforms like Zoom, Skype, or FaceTime, offer a visual and interactive form of communication that can closely mimic an in-person experience. For individuals with SAD, who might find leaving the house or engaging in social activities overwhelming during the peak of their symptoms, video calls can be a lifeline. They provide a sense of presence and connection without the need for physical travel, making it easier to maintain relationships with friends and family.

Social media platforms play a similarly vital role. They offer a space for individuals to stay connected with their social circles, share experiences, and offer support to one another. For many, these platforms can be a source of positivity and community, offering content that can uplift mood and create a sense of belonging. Social media also provides access to various support groups and forums where individuals with SAD can connect with others who share similar experiences, fostering a sense of understanding and solidarity.

Other digital platforms, such as blogs, podcasts, and online forums, offer additional resources for support and information. They can be instrumental in providing tips for managing SAD, sharing personal stories, or simply offering content that can distract and entertain during difficult times.

However, it's important to approach digital interactions mindfully. While these platforms offer numerous benefits, excessive or unregulated use of social media and digital communication can sometimes lead to increased feelings of isolation or comparison. It's therefore crucial for individuals to find a balance that works for them, ensuring that their digital interactions are healthy and beneficial to their overall well-being.

Digital platforms offer valuable means for maintaining social connections and accessing support, particularly for those affected by Seasonal Affective Disorder. They provide flexible and accessible options for interaction, which can be especially useful when traditional, face-to-face interactions are challenging. By leveraging these technological tools, individuals with SAD can maintain their social networks and support systems, which are essential components in managing the condition effectively.

Balancing Socializing with Self-Care

While socializing is beneficial, it's also important to recognize the need for personal downtime and self-care. Maintaining social connections is a vital part of managing SAD. It's important to find a balance that works for you, ensuring that while you have a supportive social network, you also have time for self-care and solitude. In the next chapters, we'll explore how to create a supportive environment at home and workplace strategies for coping with SAD.

Chapter 11: Creating a Supportive Environment

Creating a supportive environment is essential in managing Seasonal Affective Disorder (SAD). The spaces where we live and work significantly influence our mood and overall well-being. This chapter explores ways to optimize these environments to better support those with SAD.

Maximizing Natural Light

Natural light plays a crucial role in regulating our mood and circadian rhythms. To make the most of natural light, consider rearranging your living and workspaces. Position your furniture, especially areas where you spend a lot of time, near windows. Keep curtains and blinds open during the day and consider using sheer window treatments to allow more light while maintaining privacy. Regularly cleaning windows can also increase light penetration, brightening the space significantly.

Color and Décor

The choice of color in our surroundings can greatly affect our mood. Bright and light colors tend to create an uplifting and energizing atmosphere, which can be particularly beneficial during the darker months. Consider repainting walls or incorporating accessories in cheerful colors. Decorative elements like wall art, cushions, or rugs with stimulating patterns can also add vibrancy. Incorporating elements of nature, such as indoor plants or nature-inspired artwork, can bring a sense of calm and connection to the outdoors, which is often missing during the winter months.

Organizing and Decluttering

A cluttered space can contribute to feelings of stress and overwhelm. Organizing and decluttering your living and working areas can create a more peaceful and calming environment. This might involve regular tidying, investing in storage solutions, or adopting a minimalist approach to possessions. A tidy and organized space can help in maintaining a clearer, more focused mind, which is especially important when dealing with the cognitive effects of SAD.

Light Therapy at Home

For many with SAD, light therapy is a crucial component of daily routine. To encourage consistent use, create a dedicated space for light therapy that is comfortable and inviting. This could be a cozy corner with your light box, a comfortable chair, and perhaps a small table for a cup of tea or a book. Making this space appealing ensures that your light therapy session is something to look forward to rather than a chore.

Creating a Relaxing Bedroom Environment

Quality sleep is vital when managing SAD. Ensure your bedroom environment promotes restfulness. This might mean investing in blackout curtains to encourage deeper sleep, using comfortable bedding, and maintaining a cool room temperature. The bedroom should be a tech-free sanctuary, free from distractions that could disrupt sleep, such as TVs and smartphones.

Scent and Sound

The ambiance of a room can be further enhanced by engaging other senses. Aromatherapy, using scents like lavender or jasmine, can have a calming effect, reducing stress and improving mood. Similarly, having a selection of calming music, nature sounds, or white noise can create a tranquil atmosphere, conducive to relaxation and mental well-being.

Chapter 12: Seasonal Depression in Children and Adolescents

Seasonal Affective Disorder (SAD) in children and adolescents is often overlooked, yet it's important to address it for their overall mental health and development. Symptoms in young people can be different from adults, and recognizing these signs is the first step in providing support.

Recognizing the Signs

In younger individuals, SAD can manifest as irritability, mood swings, a noticeable drop in energy, difficulties in concentrating, and changes in sleep and eating patterns. Parents may also observe a decline in academic performance or a lack of interest in previously enjoyed activities. Being aware of these changes, especially their seasonal nature, is crucial for early intervention.

The Role of Parents and Caregivers

Parents and caregivers are often the first to notice signs of SAD in children. It's important for them to monitor any seasonal behavior and mood changes and seek professional help for a proper assessment. Creating an open and supportive environment where children feel comfortable discussing their feelings is vital.

Treatment Approaches for Young People

Treatment for SAD in children and adolescents may include light therapy, though it should be under the guidance of a healthcare provider. Cognitive-Behavioral Therapy (CBT), adapted for younger individuals, can be highly effective. Encouraging physical activity, especially outdoors during daylight hours, can also be beneficial. Ensuring a routine that includes sufficient sleep and a healthy diet is important in managing symptoms.

The School's Role

Schools play a critical role in supporting students with SAD. Awareness among teachers and school counselors can help in identifying students who might be struggling. Schools can provide accommodations, like flexibility with deadlines or additional support during difficult months, which can significantly alleviate stress for students experiencing SAD.

Family Support and Education

Families should be educated about SAD and its impact on young people. This includes understanding how to support a child or adolescent through lifestyle adjustments, maintaining a routine, and encouraging social interaction. Family activities that promote togetherness and outdoor time can be particularly helpful.

Chapter 13: Workplace and Seasonal Depression

Chapter 13 addresses the challenges of managing Seasonal Affective Disorder (SAD) in a professional environment. The workplace can significantly impact an individual's experience with SAD, and understanding how to navigate these challenges is crucial for maintaining productivity and well-being.

Recognizing Workplace Challenges

For those with SAD, typical workplace environments can exacerbate symptoms. Long hours indoors, limited exposure to natural light, and workplace stress can all contribute to the severity of SAD symptoms. Recognizing these factors is the first step in creating a more supportive work environment.

Adapting the Work Environment

Small changes in the workplace can make a significant difference. If possible, choose workspaces with access to natural light or request a desk near a window. Employers and employees can consider the use of light therapy devices at workstations. Ergonomic adjustments, such as comfortable seating and a pleasant, personalized workspace, can also help enhance mood and productivity.

Flexible Work Arrangements

Flexible work hours can be a valuable accommodation for individuals with SAD. Adjusting work hours to coincide with daylight hours, especially in the winter months, can be beneficial. For some, the option to work from home, where they can create a more controlled environment, may also help manage symptoms.

Communication and Support in the Workplace

Open communication with supervisors and human resource departments about the challenges of SAD is important. Employers who are informed about SAD can provide necessary support and accommodations. Building a support system among colleagues can also provide a network of understanding and assistance.

Stress Management and Self-Care

Managing workplace stress is crucial for individuals with SAD. This can include regular breaks, time management techniques, and setting realistic work goals. Prioritizing self-care, such as mindfulness practices or short walks during breaks, can also help mitigate symptoms.

Navigating SAD in the workplace requires a combination of personal strategies and supportive workplace practices. Creating an environment that acknowledges and accommodates SAD can lead to better mental health and improved work performance for those affected.

Chapter 14: Preventing and Preparing for the Seasonal Shift

Chapter 14 focuses on strategies for anticipating and mitigating the effects of Seasonal Affective Disorder (SAD) before the onset of symptoms. Proactive measures can help lessen the impact of SAD and improve overall well-being during vulnerable times of the year.

Understanding Seasonal Patterns

Being aware of personal patterns related to SAD is crucial. Tracking mood and energy levels throughout the year can help identify when symptoms typically begin and how they progress. This awareness allows for early intervention and preparation.

Lifestyle Adjustments Before the Season Change

Implementing lifestyle changes before the onset of the SAD season can be effective in reducing severity. This includes establishing a regular exercise routine, optimizing diet for mental health, and ensuring a consistent sleep schedule.

Light Therapy as a Preventive Measure

Starting light therapy before the typical onset of symptoms can help prevent their full development. For many, this means beginning light therapy in early fall.

Building a Support System

Strengthening social connections and informing friends, family, and colleagues about one's needs and challenges related to SAD can provide a supportive network during difficult months.

Mental Health Maintenance

Engaging in activities that promote mental well-being, such as mindfulness, yoga, or regular therapy sessions, can fortify emotional resilience. Developing a self-care routine that includes activities like journaling, creative hobbies, or relaxation techniques can also be beneficial.

Planning for Challenging Times

Having a plan in place for the more challenging times can make a significant difference. This might include scheduling regular check-ins with a therapist, planning enjoyable activities during the darker months, and setting realistic expectations for oneself during this period.

Preventing and preparing for the seasonal shifts associated with SAD involves a combination of understanding personal patterns, making proactive lifestyle adjustments, and establishing a supportive network.

These strategies can help smooth the transition into more difficult seasons and ensure a more balanced experience throughout the year.

Chapter 15: Beyond Winter: Year-Round Strategies for Mental Wellness

Chapter 15 emphasizes the importance of maintaining mental wellness throughout the year, not just during the peak seasons of Seasonal Affective Disorder (SAD). A holistic approach to mental health can help mitigate the impact of SAD and promote overall well-being.

Embracing a Holistic Lifestyle

Adopting a holistic approach means considering all aspects of health - physical, emotional, and social. This includes regular physical activity, a balanced diet, adequate sleep, and stress management. Such a lifestyle not only helps in managing SAD but also contributes to overall health and well-being.

Mindfulness and Relaxation Techniques

Practices such as mindfulness, meditation, and yoga can be beneficial throughout the year. These techniques help in managing stress, improving focus, and maintaining a calm and balanced state of mind.

Regular Physical Activity

Exercise is a powerful mood booster. Engaging in regular physical activity, whether it's structured exercise, outdoor activities, or just daily walks, can have profound effects on mood, energy levels, and sleep quality.

Nutrition for Mental Health

A diet rich in fruits, vegetables, whole grains, lean protein, and omega-3 fatty acids supports brain health and mood regulation. Avoiding excessive caffeine, alcohol, and processed foods can also help in maintaining stable mood and energy levels.

Building and Maintaining Social Connections

Maintaining strong social connections is vital for mental health. Regularly engaging in social activities, nurturing relationships, and seeking support when needed can provide a buffer against the symptoms of SAD.

Ongoing Therapy and Support

For those who benefit from therapy, maintaining regular sessions throughout the year can provide continuous support and help in addressing any underlying issues that may contribute to SAD. Managing SAD effectively involves more than just addressing the symptoms as they arise. It requires a commitment to year-round mental wellness through a combination of lifestyle choices, relaxation techniques, social engagement, and professional support.

Chapter 16: Resources and Support Networks

In Chapter 16, we explore the variety of resources and support networks available for individuals dealing with Seasonal Affective Disorder (SAD). Knowing where to find help and support is crucial in managing SAD effectively.

Professional Mental Health Resources

Seeking help from mental health professionals, such as therapists, counselors, or psychiatrists, is a critical step. They can provide a diagnosis, recommend treatment plans, and offer ongoing support. You can find a resource directory following chapter 16.

Support Groups

Support groups for individuals with SAD can be invaluable. These groups provide a space to share experiences, offer and receive advice, and find understanding and empathy. Support groups can be found through local mental health services, hospitals, or online platforms.

Online Resources and Forums

The internet offers a wealth of information and support. Websites, forums, and social media groups dedicated to SAD can provide helpful information, coping strategies, and a sense of community.

Educational Materials

Books, articles, and educational websites on SAD can offer insights into the disorder, treatment options, and lifestyle tips. It's important to seek out reputable sources to ensure the information is accurate and reliable.

Hotlines and Crisis Centers

For immediate help or during a crisis, hotlines and crisis centers can provide support and guidance. These services are especially important for individuals experiencing severe depression or suicidal thoughts.

Integrating Family and Friends

Educating family members and friends about SAD can help them understand the condition and how they can offer support. This can include sharing literature, discussing treatment plans, and expressing what kind of support is most helpful.

A wide range of resources and support networks is available for those dealing with SAD. Utilizing these resources can provide valuable information, support, and a sense of community, all of which are important in managing the condition effectively.

Conclusion: Embracing the Seasons of the Mind

As we reach the conclusion of our journey through understanding and managing Seasonal Affective Disorder (SAD), it's important to reflect on the key insights and strategies that have been explored. This book has aimed to provide a comprehensive understanding of SAD, delving into its symptoms, causes, and the various ways in which it manifests and affects individuals.

We began by exploring the nature of SAD, highlighting how it differs from other forms of depression and the unique challenges it presents. The significance of light, both natural and artificial, was underscored in our discussion on the science behind SAD, emphasizing the profound impact of our environment on mental health. Personal stories brought to light the varied and deeply personal experiences of those living with SAD, offering a reminder of the human aspect behind the disorder.

Key strategies for managing SAD were examined, including the pivotal role of light therapy as a cornerstone of treatment. The importance of a balanced diet, regular exercise, and maintaining hydration was discussed, noting how these lifestyle factors play a crucial role in mitigating symptoms. Cognitive-behavioral strategies and the potential use of medication were also explored, providing a toolkit of therapeutic options for those affected.

The significance of maintaining social connections, adapting the workplace environment, and preparing for seasonal changes was highlighted, offering practical advice for day-to-day living with SAD. We also delved into the less discussed aspect of SAD in children and adolescents, emphasizing the importance of early recognition and support for younger individuals.

Finally, we looked at the resources and support networks available, stressing the importance of seeking help and fostering a community of support.

In conclusion, while Seasonal Affective Disorder presents its challenges, understanding and managing this condition is well within reach. By combining knowledge with proactive management strategies, individuals affected by SAD can not only navigate the darker seasons more comfortably but can also embrace all the seasons of their lives with resilience and hope. This book is a testament to the power of understanding, the effectiveness of various treatments, and the strength found in community and support. As each season passes, may this knowledge empower you to find balance and well-being, no matter the weather outside.

National Institute of Mental Health (NIMH)

Website: www.nimh.nih.gov

Description: Provides comprehensive information on SAD, including symptoms, treatment options, and current research.

American Psychiatric Association (APA)

Website: www.psychiatry.org

Description: Offers resources and information on various mental health conditions, including SAD. Also provides guidelines for finding psychiatrists.

Mayo Clinic

Website: www.mayoclinic.org

Description: A reliable source for information on symptoms, causes, and treatment of SAD, including lifestyle and home remedies.

SAD Association (SADA)

Website: www.sada.org.uk

Description: UK's leading organization on SAD, offering advice, information, and support.

Mental Health America (MHA)

Website: www.mhanational.org

Description: Provides a wide range of mental health resources and includes a section on SAD.

Anxiety and Depression Association of America (ADAA)

Website: www.adaa.org

Description: Offers information on depression, anxiety, and related disorders, including SAD. Provides resources for finding therapists and support groups.

Psychology Today: Therapist Finder

Website: www.psychologytoday.com

Description: A tool for finding therapists, psychiatrists, support groups, and treatment facilities.

SAMHSA's National Helpline

Website: www.samhsa.gov

Hotline: 1-800-662-HELP (4357)

Description: A confidential, free, 24/7, 365-day-a-year treatment referral and information service for individuals facing mental and/or substance use disorders.

Light Therapy Product Reviews and Recommendations

Website: www.consumerreports.org

Description: Provides reviews and information on various light therapy products.

Mood Disorders Society of Canada

Website: www.mooddisorderscanada.ca

Description: Offers resources and information on mood disorders, including SAD, for Canadians.

Center for Environmental Therapeutics (CET)

Website: www.cet.org

Description: Provides information on light therapy, chronotherapy, and other environmental therapies for SAD and related conditions.

Online Support Communities

Websites like Reddit (www.reddit.com) and HealthUnlocked (www.healthunlocked.com) often have forums and support groups for individuals with SAD.